I0411099

MODULE 1

THE ROLE OF NGOS IN A CIVIL SOCIETY

In this first module of *An NGO Training Guide for Peace Corps Volunteers*, you build on your experiences with nonprofit organizations in the United States to gain an understanding of the critical role nongovernmental organizations (NGOs) play in developing civil societies. By the time you complete this module you should have acquired the knowledge, skills, and attitudes to:

- Describe four characteristics that differentiate NGOs from government organizations and for-profit businesses.

- Identify some major sectors (e.g., health, youth, or women's issues) where NGOs are active in your country of service.

- Explain in your own words how each of the six key elements of public participation increases the involvement of citizens in a civil society.

- Select three words that describe the appropriate role of a Peace Corps Volunteer in working with NGOs, and give examples of situations where each role would be useful.

A VOLUNTEER'S STORY

Peace Corps/Jamaica Volunteers work with a variety of NGOs and community-based organizations (CBOs).

An environmental business Volunteer and her Counterpart realize that there are few better ways to inspire youths' interest in the environment than by involving them in hands-on projects to improve their environment. They helped youth at the Jack's Hill Community Center organize an environmental club. The new club decided to plant ferns at Jackson Spring.

The Volunteer reports. "The following Saturday, I arrived at Jackson Spring at 8:00 a.m. to find a group of six youth brushing the spring area and preparing it for planting. I was excited to see my Counterpart and the kids had taken so much interest in the environment and that our project was underway."

Service projects involving groups of students allow young persons to learn to work together and develop leadership roles. In addition, they offer opportunities for students to analyze problems and propose and execute solutions. Through participation, youth prepare to take on citizens' responsibilities in a civil society. When students are put in positions of responsibility, they are counted on to show up on time and ready to work and to see a project through to completion. They learn the consequences of letting down those they intended to help. These "life skills" are important for later success.

* * * * * * * * * *

WHAT IS YOUR EXPERIENCE WITH NONGOVERNMENTAL ORGANIZATIONS?

Initially, you may think that your experience with NGOs has been minimal. However, consider such organizations as Big Brothers/Sisters, Boy/Girl Scouts, Goodwill, Salvation Army, YMCA, and your local church or place of worship and the extent to which they are involved in your daily life. In the United States these organizations are called nonprofits or not-for-profits; in the rest of the world they are more commonly known as nongovernmental organizations (NGOs). They play an important role in most communities.

As a Volunteer your service is likely to involve NGOs. A number of Volunteers report successful, satisfying experiences working with NGOs either in their primary assignment or through community outreach projects. Volunteers in all sectors (agriculture, business, education, environment, health, and youth) work with NGOs.

In this module, you will begin to learn more about NGOs. You will have opportunities to:

- Review and reflect on your previous experiences with nonprofit organizations;

- Read about the important role that NGOs play in development;

- Engage in short activities to explore how NGOs operate in your country of service; and

- Discover why and how PCVs work with NGOs.

Take a few moments to reflect on your experiences with nonprofit organizations. Many of you have provided services and assistance, and/or given money to these organizations. You may have donated blood to the American Red Cross. During Halloween some may have participated in the Trick-or-Treat for UNICEF (United Nations International Children's Education Fund) program that raised funds for children around the world. Others may have helped the local parent-teacher association (PTA), fraternity or sorority, Rotary Club, or the Sierra Club. And still others may have been impacted by the powerful message of a nonprofit founded by an individual with a passionate message, such as Mothers Against Drunk Driving (MADD).

"Never doubt that a small group of committed citizens can change the world. Indeed, it is the only thing that ever has."
—Margaret Mead

ACTIVITY 1:1

COMMON CHARACTERISTICS OF NGOS

In this activity, you begin the process of transferring your knowledge and understanding of nonprofits in your home country to the workings of NGOs in your country of service.

1. Choose a nonprofit organization you are familiar with and answer the following:

    *   What programs and services did the nonprofit offer?

    *   Who were their stakeholders? Individuals who cared about or benefited from the organization? Why was the organization founded? Who founded the organization?

    *   Who managed the organization: a board of directors, paid staff, volunteers?

    *   How was the organization financed: donations, special fundraising events, fees from beneficiaries, grants, or a combination of these?

    *   How did you become involved with the organization: contributor, volunteer, board member, beneficiary, or staff member?

    *   What difference would it make in the community if the nonprofit organization did not exist?

2. Share your answers about the nonprofit organization with others in your training group.

3. Can the group agree on common characteristics of nonprofit organizations?

Note: You may wish to refer to the list of possible common characteristics of nonprofit organizations at the end of this module in Activity 1:1 Reference.

WHY THE PEACE CORPS
PLACES VOLUNTEERS WITH NGOS

The Peace Corps is a unique government development agency with a history of working with community partners and colleagues to build capacity one person at a time. From its beginnings, the Peace Corps' philosophy has been that it is better to teach people to fish or raise their own fish than to give them fish to eat. This is what capacity building is about—empowering people to help themselves. Today, Volunteers continue to build individual capacity and the capacity of organizations and communities.

Increasingly, NGOs are recognized as important players in the formulation, design, and application of development strategies. International development organizations are placing greater emphasis on working with national and local NGOs to emphasize local knowledge and participatory development

The Peace Corps' development philosophy is similar to the philosophy of many NGOs. Ideally, a Peace Corps' project should:

- Increase local capacities;

- Target beneficiaries who are often among the needy;

- Seek sustainable solutions; and

- Involve beneficiaries in the development process.

When the interests of the Peace Corps and an NGO overlap, working together helps both organizations achieve their goals.

However, some NGOs' missions do not coincide with those of the Peace Corps. For example, the Peace Corps does not place Volunteers with an NGO whose mission is to elect political candidates, or an NGO with countercultural values. In many countries this is a very delicate balance. The Peace Corps strives to support civil societies, and NGOs generally contribute to building civil societies. Yet, in some countries NGOs question governmental authority and thus are seen as destabilizing influences.

"I know of no more encouraging fact than the unquestionable ability of man to elevate his life by conscious endeavor."

——Henry David Thoreau

CHARACTERISTICS THAT DISTINGUISH NGOS

An organization may be correctly labeled an NGO if it has four characteristics identified by The Commonwealth Foundation, a London-based NGO study group. These characteristics are included here, with the permission of The Commonwealth Foundation, from its 1995 publication *Non-Governmental Organizations: Guidelines for Good Policy and Practice.*

1. **Voluntary:** NGOs are formed voluntarily by citizens with an element of voluntary participation in the organization, whether in the form of small numbers of board members or large numbers of members or time given by volunteers.

2. **Independent:** NGOs are independent within the laws of society, and controlled by those who have formed them or by elected or appointed boards. The legal status of NGOs is based on freedom of association—one of the most basic human rights. The International Covenant of Civil and Political Rights, developed by the United Nations in 1966 and since ratified by 135 countries, grants the right to assemble.

3. **Not-for-profit:** NGOs are not for private personal profit or gain. NGOs may, in many countries, engage in revenue-generating activities, but must use the revenue solely in pursuit of the organization's mission. Like other enterprises, NGOs have employees who are paid for what they do. Boards are not usually paid for the work they perform, but may be reimbursed for expenses they incur in the course of performing their board duties.

4. **Not self-serving in aims and related values:** The aims of NGOs are to improve the circumstances and prospects of people and to act on concerns and issues detrimental to the well-being, circumstances, or prospects of people or society as a whole.

NGOs are not the only name used to describe organizations that have the four characteristics listed above. Other common names are listed in the chart below. You may notice that the names reflect one of the distinguishing characteristics of the group.

NAME	CHARACTERISTICS
Nonprofit or Not-for-profit Organization	The organization's goal is not to make a profit for the benefit of organizers, but can earn money to achieve the organization's mission.
Private Voluntary Organization (PVO) and Voluntary Sector	Acknowledges the importance of volunteers and voluntary action.
Independent Sector or the Third Sector	Distinguishes organizations from the business or government sectors.
Philanthropic Sector or Charitable Organization	Addresses the charitable nature of these organizations.
Social Sector	Underscores how the activities of this class of organizations enhance the social fabric of a country.
Community-Based Organization (CBO)	Stresses the participation of and benefit for local citizens.
Civil Society Organization (CSO)	An emerging and increasingly popular name that focuses on a desired outcome of these groups—the creation of a civil society.

"There can be hope only for a society
which acts as one big family,
and not as many separate ones."

—Anwar Sadat (1918–1981),
President of Egypt

Organizations usually belong to one of three sectors of society: the government sector, for-profit/private business sector, and the NGO/third sector.

For a society to achieve its full potential and for citizens to fulfill their goals, all three sectors must cooperate with one another. Each sector has strengths and weaknesses in providing what citizens need and want.

- The business sector most effectively delivers goods.

- The government sector drafts and enforces laws, and defends the country's borders.

- The third sector, which consists of nongovernmental organizations, provides services that the business and government sectors are unwilling or unable to provide, and they provide a venue for citizens to come together and be heard on issues that they feel are important.

It is not easy to identify which of the sectors an organization belongs to. When a business exerts significant influence over an NGO's operations, the term business-organized NGO (BONGO) is used. Governments often contract with NGOs to provide certain public services. If a government exerts significant influence over an NGO, it is called a government-organized NGO (GONGO) or quasi-nongovernmental organization (QUANGO). The divisions get fuzzy; it is often difficult to determine when an NGO is independent of a business or government partner and when its partner, in fact, controls the NGO.

In most NGO/business and NGO/government partnerships, the NGO retains its independence. For example, the Ford Foundation and the Soros Foundation are well known. These organizations engage in charitable activities and administer research grants while taking advantage of the tax law benefits. These foundations operate independently of the founding business; they are not BONGOs.

You are likely to encounter additional local language(s) names for NGO-type organizations.

Beyond providing services, a second and perhaps more important function of NGOs is as a facilitator of citizens' participation in their societies. NGOs enable all voices to be heard when individuals form a group with others who have similar values and interests. NGOs often aim to promote understanding between citizens and the state.

NGOs contribute to a civil society by providing a means for expressing and actively addressing the varied and complex needs of society. They are seen as serving several essential functions:

- NGOs promote pluralism, diversity, and tolerance in society while protecting and strengthening cultural, ethnic, religious, linguistic, and other identities.

- NGOs advance science and thought; develop culture and art; protect the environment; and support all activities and concerns that make a vibrant civil society.

- NGOs motivate citizens in all aspects of society to act, rather than depend on state power and beneficence.

- NGOs create an alternative to centralized state agencies and provide services with greater independence and flexibility.

NGOs establish the mechanisms by which governments and the market can be held accountable by the public.

Why are NGOs important? The short answer: NGOs increase "social capital" by providing people with opportunities to build trust in each other and the capacity to work together toward common goals.

In recent years the presence and number of NGOs has grown. However, the influence and importance of NGOs differ depending on the national context in which they operate.

What follows are a few examples of the focus and scale of NGOs in countries where Volunteers have served or are serving:

- In Jordan, local NGOs enjoy royal patronage, and many work with youth and women's issues.

- Kenya has more than 600 NGOs, many working in grass-roots community development.

- In the Philippines, 500,000 registered Philippine NGOs try to make a difference in a variety of sectors, including AIDS education and environmental preservation.

- In Russia, NGOs deliver business services, assist battered women, and work on environment education.

- In Slovakia, there are more than 350 NGOs, many working toward the development of an effective civil society.

ACTIVITY 1:2

LEARNING ABOUT LOCAL NGOS

Discuss with other trainees, language instructors, and/or technical trainers the best methods for learning about NGOs in your host country: individual discussions; field trips to NGOs; panel discussions with NGO staff; Volunteers working with NGOs and their Counterparts; reading articles about local NGOs. Develop a plan to gather the information you need.

Below are questions to help you learn about NGOs in your host country.

1. How many different NGOs can you identify that are active in your host country?

2. How does the work differ for each organization?

3. What kind of work could Volunteers do with each organization?

4. What is the historical, cultural, and economic context of NGOs in your host country?

5. When were NGOs developed in the country—after independence, after Communism?

6. What are the political ramifications of NGOs in the country? What are the sensitivities, issues, and concerns?

7. How do most NGOs receive their financial support? What implication does this have on how NGOs work in the country? How do the economics of your host country affect NGOs?

8. Are NGOs a cultural norm? Are they new to the cultural landscape? What are the ramifications of their position in society?

9. Why are NGOs important to the country's development? Do they play a significant role?

10. What is/are the local language name(s) used to describe NGO-type organizations?

WHAT CONSTITUTES A CIVIL SOCIETY

What constitutes a civil society varies from culture to culture. A civil society can be defined by one culture in terms of the results or behaviors produced. Another definition may focus on the preconditions or foundations for civil society. A third culture may describe it as a desirable state for all society. And a fourth may emphasize the composition of civil society—who is and is not included. Within these four broad categories are many variations. Another consideration in discussing civil society is the cultural context. What are considered essential elements for a civil society in one culture may not be essential elements in another culture.

Determine what local citizens consider key elements of a civil society. The following elements reflect a Western point of view and can serve as a starting point for a conversation with citizens of your host country. These elements are thought to promote an active, inclusive, and diversified public participation process.

1. The government is proactive in expanding opportunities for public participation. All individuals have the right to be part of the decisions influencing their quality of life.

2. Special efforts are made to include women, indigenous people, youth, and other traditionally marginalized groups, such as disadvantaged racial and ethnic minorities. Being inclusive involves engaging the for-profit business and government sectors. Being inclusive is fundamental to achieving long-term solutions that are equitable and therefore sustainable.

3. The three sectors of society share responsibilities to ensure public participation. Effective partnerships between NGOs and/or businesses and government require concerted efforts to become and remain accountable, transparent, and inclusive.

4. Continuous public participation throughout the process of design, implementation, and evaluation of projects, policies, or programs legitimizes decisions and enriches outcomes.

5. Transparency ensures all motives and objectives are apparent and information vital to a decision is presented and is reliable.

6. Cooperation among national, regional, and local government authorities and NGOs is essential for effective coordination of public participation. It is not sufficient to have cooperation at only one or even two levels.

7. Openness to informal as well as formal routes of communication broadens the scope of public participation.

In a developing civil society, an ever-increasing number of people are involved in all types of activities and decisions. These citizens come from all the different parts of the society and represent its diversity. Each country, including the

United States, is at a different place on the continuum of a "developed" civil society. None is a society in which all citizens participate on a regular basis.

NGOs are strengthening the fabric of civil societies in still-fragile, emerging democracies. They are essential partners for governments, the private sector, and development organizations in meeting people's needs. NGOs are an expression of people's belief that through their own initiative, they can better fulfill their potential by working together, and in so doing reduce the opportunity gap that exists between the advantaged and disadvantaged in society.

"Courage happens when people unite."

—Anonymous

ACTIVITY 1:3

ANALYZING PROGRESS TOWARD ACHIEVING A CIVIL SOCIETY

Organize a diverse focus group of five or six local citizens, including old/young, men/women, and members from different social or ethnic groups. You should ask people who trust you to take part—perhaps host family members or friends.

A training participant can act as facilitator. Briefly explain what the term civil society means to an American, then appreciatively ask the following questions. Each member of the focus group should be given the opportunity to voice an opinion. Do not force group members to speak.

- What do you consider the essential elements of a civil society? Are some elements more important than others?

- What progress has your country made in developing a civil society?

- What groups actively participate in the decision-making process?

- Which groups are not allowed or encouraged to participate?

- What efforts are being made to increase public participation?

- Who is making efforts to achieve participation?

Reflect on the information you have gathered either individually or in small groups.

- What did you learn about civil society in your host country?

- What is the level of participation (use voting, community involvement, and volunteer activities as a benchmark)?

- What are the implications to your work as a Volunteer?

- How does a heightened awareness of the importance of participation affect how you plan to function as a Volunteer?

HOW PEACE CORPS VOLUNTEERS
WORK WITH NGOs

Earlier in this module, you reflected on your experiences with nonprofit organizations in the United States and investigated how NGOs operate in your host country. You explored the important role NGOs play in a civil society through reading, activities, and discussions. Now it is time to discuss the role of Volunteers in working with NGOs.

What are Volunteers expected to accomplish and how are they expected to accomplish it? The "what" is about results. The "how" is about process.

Some Volunteers assist NGOs with organizational development—basic computer literacy, learning English, and building financial, human, and program capacities. Other Volunteers are directly involved in the delivery of services—AIDS education, youth programs, environmental awareness, etc. Many Volunteers report that they become involved in both organizational development and service delivery.

"What" specifically you do in working with an NGO depends on the interaction of three things:

1. your interest, skills, and expectations;

2. what types of assistance the NGO needs; and

3. how the first two fit with the goals of your Peace Corps project.

The how, not the what, is often more difficult. It is generally easier to figure out what needs to be done than how to do it.

Catalyst, facilitator, coach, mentor, partner, and learner are words that describe how. Exactly which word(s) denotes the right role(s) for you as a Volunteer depends on your personal style and the work style of your NGO Counterparts.

A catalyst is a change agent. Catalysts speed up a reaction, but are not used up in the reaction. A Volunteer who acts as a catalyst has a similar role, suggesting how changes can occur smoothly and quickly. A catalyst Volunteer generates ideas and networks to make links with other organizations. Some of the Volunteer's ideas will be picked up and implemented. Most will not. This is a good "how" role when the NGO staff have basic skills but are discouraged from working in a tough regulatory, economic, and/or cultural environment.

A facilitator acts as a guide, helping the group achieve their agreed-on goals effectively. A facilitator balances achieving results with learning from the process. If the process moves too slowly, some in the group become impatient to see the results; if the process moves too quickly, others are frustrated that the project is not being carefully thought out and creative options explored. Experience shows that more capacity building takes place during the process than through results.

A coach aims to enhance the performance and learning ability of others. Coaching involves feedback, motivation, effective questioning, and consciously matching your style to a person's readiness to undertake a particular task. It is based on helping people to help themselves. A good "how" role when you need to teach skills.

A mentor is similar to a coach, with some slight differences. A mentor is usually older or more experienced than the person being mentored. There is a high level of trust between the person being mentored and the mentor. A mentor often provides emotional support as well as coaching technical skills. A good "how" role for an experienced Volunteer and certain individual staff members at the NGO.

A partner is an equal. Partners may have complementary skills. They share. A good "how" role for you when working with an individual whose skill level is nearly equal to yours, but whose skills may be different.

A learner asks people what they do, how they do it, when and where they do it, why they do it that way, and how he/she can help them do it better. A learner is the best "how" role during your first three months at the site. The role of a learner is always appropriate. Almost every Returned Peace Corps Volunteer says, "I learned more than I taught."

* * * * * * * * * *

In this module you have explored:

The role NGOs play as one of the three sectors in a society,

The concept of a "civil society," and

How and why Volunteers work with NGOs.

The other four modules in this manual provide additional information, useful tools, and activities to help you develop your capacity to work with NGOs.

* * * * * * * * * *

KEY TERMS

Key terms are defined as they are used in the module. A space is provided to write the translation of a word or phrase into the local language. Work with your language teachers to find the right translations and build your technical vocabulary as you study this module.

Capacity is the ability to put an idea into action.

....

Capacity building is the process of increasing the ability of an individual, organization, or community to put an idea into action.

....

Civil society generally consists of organizations that fall between the family and the state. A civil society is characterized by active, diverse, inclusive citizen participation. Political organizations and for-profit businesses are usually not considered civil society organizations.

....

Community-based organizations (CBOs) are those whose mission is primarily focused to meet a specific social or human service need within a given community. The need may be a national concern as well. In fact, the CBO may be part of a national association. CBOs tend to be more focused on a community and more informally organized than NGOs.

....

Nongovernmental organization (NGO) is the most common name used internationally for an organization formed to help others. NGOs are not governmental organizations or for-profit businesses.

....

Social capital is the ability of people to trust each other enough to work together toward agreed-on goals.

....

* * * * * * * * *

RESOURCES

These resources are available through the Peace Corps Information Collection and Exchange (ICE). The citations are presented as they appear in *The Whole ICE Catalog.*

> *Roles of the Volunteer in Development: Toolkits for Capacity Building.* (Peace Corps ICE.) 2002. 225 pp. (ICE No. T0005)
>
> This unique publication is a series of toolkits that can be separated into seven booklets. The introductory booklet provides an overview of the Peace Corps' philosophy of development, introduces the capacity-building roles a Volunteer might play, and then provides guidance for Volunteers in identifying what roles they will play. The other six booklets each address one of the roles: Learner, Co–Trainer, Co–Facilitator, Mentor, Change Agent, and Co–Planner. In each booklet, there is a chart delineating the knowledge, skills, and attitudes needed for the role; background readings on the role; and activities to learn more about and gain skills in carrying out the role. The booklets can be used as self-study, or used in conjunction with training sessions.

Internet:

www.idn.org – a source for information on NGOs and development

ACTIVITY 1:1 Reference

INFORMATION

Nonprofit organizations address a variety of people's needs and interests. The following is a sample of common characteristics of nonprofit organizations.

Nonprofits address a variety of people's needs and interests:

- People participate voluntarily in these organizations.

- Boards of directors, staff, and/or volunteers who give their time manage these organizations.

- The organization fundraises or solicits donations from people and other organizations that care about the nonprofit's mission.

- Each organization provides targeted programs and/or services to focus on its constituents' needs or interests.

- The organizations are independent and are generally known for "the good work" they do.

TRAINER'S NOTES

MODULE1:
THE ROLE OF NGOS IN A CIVIL SOCIETY

Overview:

This module allows participants to build on their experiences with nonprofit organizations in the United States to gain an understanding of the critical role that nongovernmental organizations (NGOs) play in developing civil societies. Volunteers and trainees can better appreciate why so many Volunteers work with NGOs as they begin to understand the nature of NGOs and how these organizations contribute to the well-being of society.

Time to Complete Module:

Reading	1 hour
Activities (including field trip) and debriefing activities	7 hours

Materials:

Copies of Module 1 for each training participant, blank journals, copies of relevant local NGO articles, copies of articles on citizen participation, flip chart paper, and assorted markers for each small group of training participants.

Preparation:

• Review the module and adapt readings and activities to better fit the local NGO environment and training logistics.

• Gather local information on NGOs from newspapers, magazines, and books. Translate materials if needed. Work with the language instructors to determine if some of the NGO information can be incorporated into language classes.

• Design a training plan for the module that includes how materials will be copied and distributed to trainees and arrangements for field trips and/or guest speakers.

• Display a training schedule in a location accessible to training participants and training staff. Include time for activities, debriefings, and meeting with trainees to assess the extent to which the module's learning objectives have been achieved.

• Check with the country director to determine if guidelines for Volunteers working with NGOs have been drafted. If not, work with post staff to

Continued

complete local guidelines. Because of country-specific issues, generic NGO guidelines do not suffice. See "Guidelines for Placing Volunteers with NGOs" in the Trainer's Notes section of the Introduction.

- Schedule a time to discuss with trainees what they have learned from reading Module 1 and completing the activities. Are they confident they have achieved all of the learning objectives? If not, what questions remain? What additional experiences or materials would be useful in filling any gaps in learning?

*   *   *   *   *   *   *   *   *

Both Volunteers and Counterparts benefit from an understanding of a post's guidelines for working with NGOs. After training participants finish this first module, you may want to discuss post's guidelines for working with NGOs. Another option is to defer the discussion until the end of the NGO training.

TRAINER'S NOTES

ACTIVITY1:1
COMMON CHARACTERISTICS OF NGOS

Overview:

This activity is designed to remind training participants of their experiences with nonprofits, assist them in reflecting on the critical role nonprofits play in a community, and help them identify some common characteristics of a nonprofit organization.

Time: 1 hour

Materials:

Flip chart and markers.

Preparation:

Identify a time and a place where training participants can meet to discuss their experiences with nonprofit organizations and discuss common characteristics of nonprofit organizations. Select a training participant to facilitate the group discussion.

Debriefing the experience and processing the learnings:

Encourage training participants to draw on their experiences and reflect on what they know about nonprofit organizations. The next step in the Experiential Learning Cycle is for the small group to generalize: "what are the common characteristics" of these organizations?

The following is a sample of some common characteristics of nonprofits:

- Address a variety of people's needs and interests.

- People participate voluntarily in these organizations.

- Managed by boards of directors who volunteer their time.

- Fundraise or solicit donations from people and other organizations that care about the nonprofit's mission.

- Provide targeted programs and/or services to focus on constituents' needs or interests.

- Independent and generally known for "the good work" they do.

TRAINER'S NOTES

ACTIVITY1:2
LEARNING ABOUT LOCAL NGOS

Overview:

This activity is designed to promote an understanding of local NGO realities from the NGOs' perspective.

Time:

Depends on activities selected by training participants and trainers.

Materials:

You may want to gather brochures or written information from NGOs visited, presenters, and other sources.

Preparation:

Local information resources will determine the best methods for gathering information about indigenous NGOs.

Debriefing the experience and processing the learnings:

After gathering information, get feedback from training participants to ensure the information collected is accurate. Discuss any misconceptions. Try answering these questions:

- What are the key learnings?

- What major challenges do local NGOs face?

- What are the implications when Volunteers work with NGOs in this country?

TRAINER'S NOTES

ACTIVITY1:3
ANALYZING PROGRESS TOWARD ACHIEVING A CIVIL SOCIETY

Overview:

This activity explores and reflects on the country's progress toward becoming a civil society.

Time: 2 hours

Materials:

Handouts on the "state" of local public participation. Provide trainees with translations of relevant media articles and/or have the language instructors use local language articles in their classes.

Debriefing the experience and processing the learnings:

The questions in this activity should generate a lively discussion. The activity is intended not to judge, but to promote an inquiry into values around and generate a discussion on the concept of a civil society and what is happening locally to develop a civil society. All countries have areas of their civil society that can be improved.

To reflect on the information that has been gathered, discuss the following questions.

• What are the major learnings about civil society in your host country?

• What is the level of participation (use voting, community involvement, and volunteer activities as benchmarks)?

• What are the implications to your work as a Volunteer?

• How does a heightened awareness of the importance of participation affect how you plan to function as a Volunteer?

www.ingramcontent.com/pod-product-compliance
Lightning Source LLC
Chambersburg PA
CBHW080405290526
45790CB00009BA/3709